ARCTIC ANIMAL MIGRATION

Migration is when an animal travels between two places it calls home. The act of migration is called migrating.

Did You Know?

Animals migrate based on which season it is.

Animals sometimes migrate because one place doesn't have everything they need to survive.

Animals might migrate to find food, have their young, or avoid harsh environments.

Harp seals migrate south in the winter. They migrate to the same places every year to have their young, which are called pups.

Did You Know?

Belugas migrate in groups called pods.

Belugas migrate south when sea ice starts to form in the fall. They migrate so they don't get trapped in ice.

Caribou on Nunavut's mainland migrate south when it gets cold. They spend the winter in forested places.

Did You Know?

Caribou on some of Nunavut's islands live on the tundra all year.

Polar bears migrate when the sea ice melts. They migrate from the ice to land so they can find food.

Snow buntings migrate south to avoid Arctic winters. They return every spring to have their young, which are called chicks.

Did You Know?

The Arctic and Antarctica have summer and winter at opposite times.

Arctic terns migrate to the other side of the world! They chase summer by going to Antarctica when it is winter in the Arctic.

Not all Arctic animals migrate. Arctic animals have found many ways to survive.

Siksiks don't migrate. They hibernate during the winter instead.

Hibernation means sleeping through a season.

Muskoxen don't hibernate or migrate to survive winter. Their thick coats keep them warm, and they have sharp hooves to dig for plants.

Animals have learned many ways to survive in the Arctic. Migration is one important tool they use!